Learning About
the Bible

Lois Rock

Illustrated by Maureen Galvani

WARNER Faith

A Division of AOL Time Warner Book Group

Acknowledgments: Bible extracts on page 12 from Mark 12:29–33 (Good News Bible) and from John 15:12 (adapted). Scriptures quoted from the Good News Bible published by The Bible Societies/HarperCollins Publishers Ltd, UK © American Bible Society 1966, 1971, 1976, 1992, used with permission.

Text by Lois Rock
Text copyright © 2003 by Lion Publishing
Illustrations copyright © 2002 Maureen Galvani

First U.S. Edition
First published in Great Britain in 2002 by Lion Publishing

ISBN 0-316-76696-8

10 9 8 7 6 5 4 3 2 1

Printed in Singapore

The text was set in Apollo MT, and the display type is Elroy and Fineprint.

Introduction: What is the Bible?

The Bible is the book of our Christian faith: the Christian Scriptures.

Not all Bibles look the same. Some are small, others are big.

Some have pictures, others only words.

Some look worn out because they are read so often. Others are kept very safe and special but are hardly read.

This book will tell you more about the Bible and what we believe about it.

1. What is the Bible?

The Bible is a collection of more than sixty very old books.

The books were all written a long time ago, in the languages of a long time ago, and it is these books that make the Bible.

Most Bibles you will see are translations— the words are in the language you speak.

In other countries, people have translations in their languages.

Some scholars have Bibles in the old languages: Hebrew, Aramaic, and Greek.

We believe that the words of the Bible are very special.

2. Why do some Bibles have pictures?

Many Bibles these days have pictures in them. The pictures are much more modern than the words. They have been added for all sorts of reasons.

Pictures help us find interesting stories to read.

Pictures help us imagine what the events looked like.

Pictures make the Bible more enjoyable for some of us who find it hard to read the words.

We make the Bible easy for everyone to enjoy and use.

3. What is a children's Bible?

There are all kinds of children's Bibles.

Some are translations of all of the Bible, but the words are specially chosen to be easy for children.

Many are retellings of the most memorable stories, and most have pictures with lots to look at. They help children begin to learn what is in the Bible.

We want children to know and enjoy the Bible.

4. What sorts of stories are in the Bible?

The Bible has all kinds of stories. Some of these are stories from long ago—the sort of stories that parents tell their children, who will later tell their children.

There are old, old stories of how God made the world and everything in it: the creation stories.

There is the old story of Noah. God told him to build an ark to save himself and his family and the animals from a great flood that would wash away all the bad things in the world.

 We believe that we can learn from all the Bible stories, even the very old ones.

5. Are the Bible stories pretend or real?

Some of the Bible stories are about real things that happened in history. People who dig up treasures from the past have found carvings and pictures and writings that tell of the same events.

Of course, when you tell a story about something that happened to you, you tell it your way.

Someone else who was with you would tell it his or her way.

The stories in the Bible are told as the Jewish people saw things: with God leading them through good times and bad times.

 We believe that the Bible tells real stories about people seeing God at work in the real world.

6. Is the story of Noah's ark true?

The Bible stories are all very old. Stories such as Noah's ark are so old that there is no one alive who knows exactly what happened. That is why people made sure to write them down.

Think about a story—any story—you know about a child who does something naughty and who learns a lesson. People in biblical times needed to learn lessons just like we do today. The Bible stories help us learn those important lessons.

We believe all the stories have important lessons. We believe that the people who wrote the Bible were inspired by God.

 We believe that the Bible stories say true things about what God is like and what people are like.

7. Is Jesus in the Bible?

Jesus is the name of the one we Christians follow. Four of the books in the Bible are all about Jesus.

These four books are called the Gospels. They are each named after the person who we believe wrote them: Matthew, Mark, Luke, and John.

The books are all a bit different. Luke tells how an angel announced the birth of Jesus and said he was God's Son. Matthew tells of wise men from far away who came to bring the baby Jesus gifts.

All the Gospels describe Jesus telling wise stories, teaching people about God, and working miracles such as calming a storm on a big lake.

All the Gospels say that Jesus was put to death on a cross. All the Gospels say that Jesus' followers believed he rose from the dead.

We read the **Bible** to learn about **Jesus** and to learn how to follow him.

8. Which story comes first: Noah's ark or Jesus?

The Bible has two big sections. The first one is called the Old Testament. The story of Noah's ark is one of the oldest in the Old Testament and comes very near the beginning.

The Old Testament is the collection of Scriptures that Jesus knew — the Scriptures of the Jewish people in Jesus' day and in our day.

The second section is called the New Testament. It is made up of the Gospels—the books about Jesus—and more books about the first Christians.

The story of Noah's ark comes a long way before the story of Jesus, and there are lots of stories in between.

 We think that the old **Scriptures** that Jesus knew and the new **Scriptures** that tell about Jesus are very important and precious.

9. How many stories are there altogether?

There are hundreds of stories! It is hard to say how many, because sometimes it is hard to say where one story ends and another begins. Some people say that all the many stories make one big story about God and God's people.

Also, there is more to the Bible than stories.

There are books that give the laws or rules God's people tried to obey.

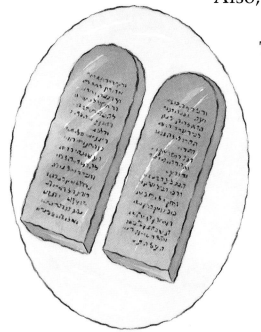

There are books with wise sayings and proverbs and hymns and poems and prayers.

There are books by the prophets—people
God chose to give his messages to
others. Sometimes the messages are
warnings and sometimes promises.

There are letters written by
Christians to people who were
learning how to follow Jesus,
giving help and advice.

 We study all the kinds of writing in the Bible
for all kinds of wisdom.

10. How do people find the parts they want to read in such a long book?

It can be hard finding the part of a book you want to read. A long time ago, when people were making copies of the Bible, someone had a smart idea.

The Bible was already written in books, each with a special name.

This person marked each book into chapters and gave each chapter a number.

This person then divided each chapter into tiny sections called verses, and each verse was given a number.

You can find anything in the Bible by finding the book, the chapter, and the verse.

The story of Noah's ark is in the first book of the Old Testament: Genesis. It begins in chapter 6, verse 5.

Luke's story of the birth of Jesus is in the Gospel of Luke, in the New Testament. It begins in chapter 2, verse 1.

We have prepared the Bible so that it is easy to find every last detail.

11. Do people have to treat the Bible in a special way?

The Bible is often called the Holy Bible. We believe that it is holy because it is the Word of God.

As a result, the Bible itself reminds us of God. So, if we hold a Bible and make a promise, it seems to make the promise even more important. It is as if we are making the promise before God.

We treat every copy of the Bible very respectfully, to show our respect for God.

When we are respectful of the book, we keep it safe. But we also show respect by reading it often, even if the book itself gets a bit worn.

 **We believe that the Bible is the holy Word of God.**

12. What is the most important thing in the Bible?

Jesus was once asked a question like this. As his answer, he told of two laws or commandments from the Old Testament.

Jesus said, "The most important one is this: 'Listen! The Lord our God is the only Lord. Love the Lord your God with all your heart, with all your soul, with all your mind, and with all your strength.' The second most important commandment is this: 'Love your neighbor as you love yourself.' There is no other commandment more important than these two."

Just before Jesus died, he gave his followers a new commandment to remember always:

"Love one another. As I have loved you, so you must love one another."

 We believe that the Bible tells us to love God and our fellow human beings.

What is the Bible?

1. We believe that the words of the Bible are very special.

2. We make the Bible easy for everyone to enjoy and use.

3. We want children to know and enjoy the Bible.

4. We believe we can learn from all the Bible stories, even the very old ones.

5. We believe that the Bible tells real stories about people seeing God at work in the real world.

6. We believe that the Bible stories say true things about what God is like and what people are like.

7. We read the Bible to learn about Jesus and to learn how to follow him.

8. We think that the old Scriptures that Jesus knew and the new Scriptures that tell about Jesus are very important and precious.

9. We study all the kinds of writing in the Bible for all kinds of wisdom.

10. We have prepared the Bible so that it is easy to find every last detail.

11. We believe that the Bible is the holy Word of God.

12. We believe that the Bible tells us to love God and our fellow human beings.